Songs of STEPHEN FOSTER

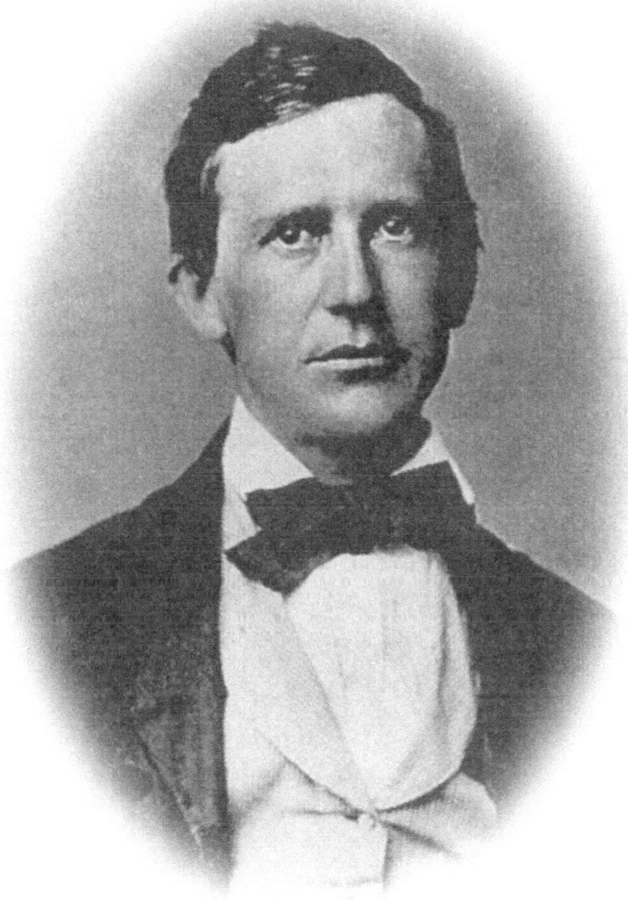

T0042538

ISBN 978-0-7935-9122-0

7777 W. Bluemound Rd. P.O. Box 13819 Milwaukee, WI 53213

Visit Hal Leonard Online at
www.halleonard.com

Stephen Foster, circa 1859-1860.

(Courtesy of the Foster Hall Collection,
Center for American Music, University of Pittsburgh Library System.)

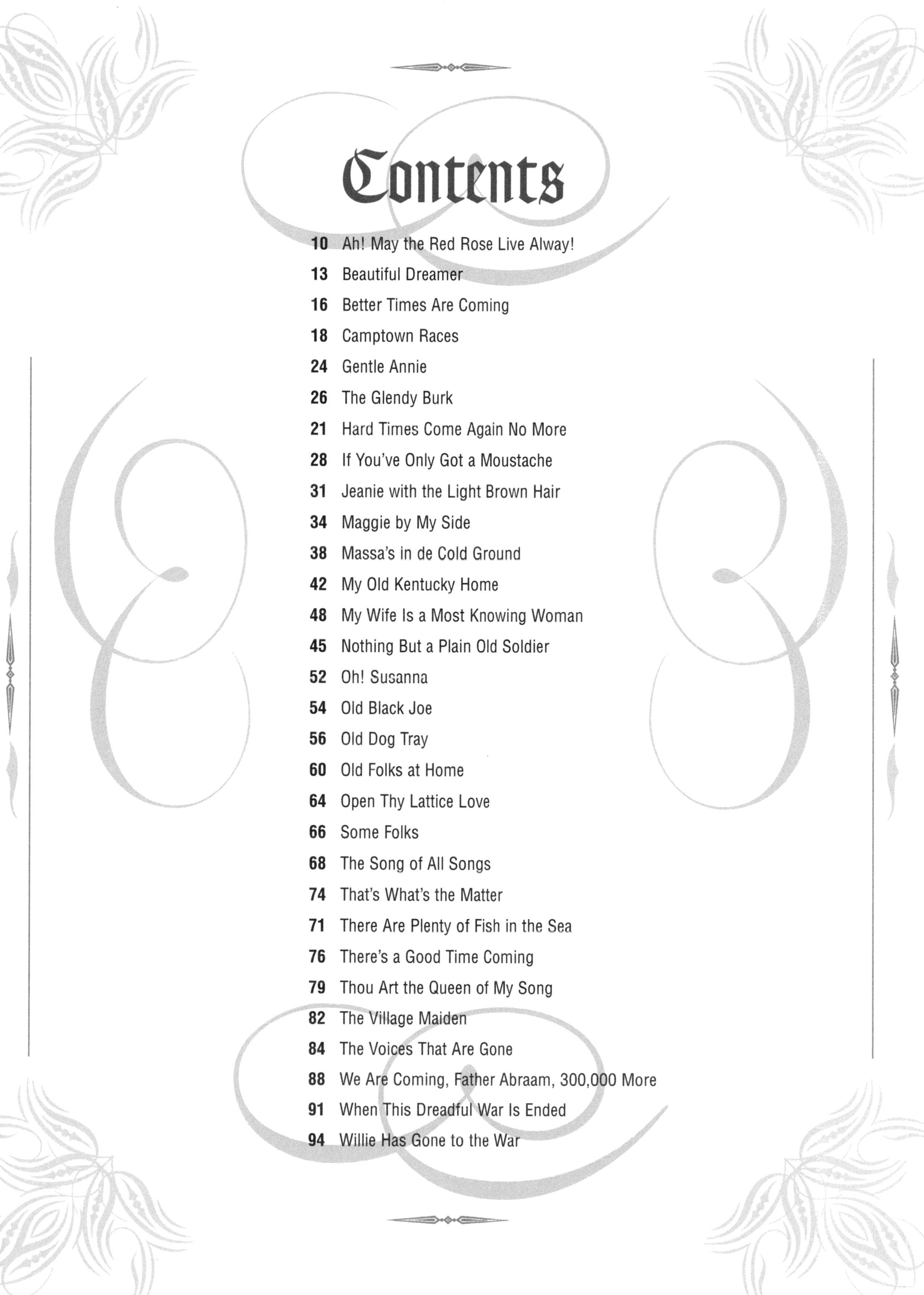

Contents

10 Ah! May the Red Rose Live Alway!
13 Beautiful Dreamer
16 Better Times Are Coming
18 Camptown Races
24 Gentle Annie
26 The Glendy Burk
21 Hard Times Come Again No More
28 If You've Only Got a Moustache
31 Jeanie with the Light Brown Hair
34 Maggie by My Side
38 Massa's in de Cold Ground
42 My Old Kentucky Home
48 My Wife Is a Most Knowing Woman
45 Nothing But a Plain Old Soldier
52 Oh! Susanna
54 Old Black Joe
56 Old Dog Tray
60 Old Folks at Home
64 Open Thy Lattice Love
66 Some Folks
68 The Song of All Songs
74 That's What's the Matter
71 There Are Plenty of Fish in the Sea
76 There's a Good Time Coming
79 Thou Art the Queen of My Song
82 The Village Maiden
84 The Voices That Are Gone
88 We Are Coming, Father Abraam, 300,000 More
91 When This Dreadful War Is Ended
94 Willie Has Gone to the War

Stephen Foster

(1826-1864)

by Elaine Schmidt

POPULAR PIONEER

Amid the maze of legends surrounding Stephen Foster's life, one fact is certain: Foster was America's first professional popular songwriter. More importantly, he created the first truly American popular music at a time when the young nation was still relying heavily on the folk music and traditions brought to its shores by its immigrant population. Long before the advent of radio and recordings or the existence of a commercial music industry, many of Foster's songs sold by the tens of thousands of copies, carried across the country and into Europe by traveling minstrel troupes. In his most successful years, Foster's songwriting brought in annual earnings of over $1,700, quite a sum for the mid-nineteenth century.

Yet by the time of his death, at age 38, America had forgotten Stephen Foster — or so it seemed. In his last years only "Old Black Joe," written in 1860, became a hit during his lifetime. But his music never disappeared. In 1928 the state of Kentucky adopted "My Old Kentucky Home," which was written in 1853, as its official state song. It is still played today at the annual running of the Kentucky Derby. In 1940, when American broadcasters and the American Society of Composers, Authors, and Publishers (ASCAP) were caught up in a heated dispute over song rights and royalties, Foster's "Jeanie with the Light Brown Hair" hit the airwaves. Written in 1854, the song was safely outside the control of the twentieth century music industry and could be played with no question of ownership or royalties. Not only did the song find a new audience, it gained the distinction of becoming one of the few songs in history, if not the only song, to make it to the Hit Parade eighty-seven years after it was written.

Foster's story, like that of many famous figures of American history, has become equal parts legend and fact through the years. It is true that Stephen Collins Foster was born on July Fourth, 1826, the day the country celebrated the fiftieth anniversary of the signing of the Declaration of Independence. It was also the day on which John Adams and Thomas Jefferson, the country's second and third presidents, died. The creator of "My Old Kentucky Home" was not, as some of the legends tell it, born to a genteel family in the South. He was born in Lawrenceville, Pennsylvania, a "suburb" of what was then a very gritty, industrial Pittsburgh. Foster's father was an entrepreneurial sort who suffered financial loss after loss, finally leading to his declaration of bankruptcy. Throughout Foster's childhood the family moved frequently, in many cases crowding into unsuitable accommodations. The youngster was often shuttled off to live with relatives while the family sorted out its domestic situation.

Although Foster showed an interest in music and an aptitude for it from a young age, his family was never able or inclined to provide him with formal training. He taught himself to play the flute and a number of other instruments,

picking up what musical information he could at the various schools he attended over the years. In pragmatic, industrial America of the nineteenth century, music was not considered a suitable career for a young man. In fact, most of polite society deemed a proficiency at music to be a harmless woman's pastime. Foster was undeterred. He was fourteen when his first song, "The Tioga Waltz," was given its premiere performance with Foster playing the lead in an arrangement for three or four flutes. The young man's songwriting began in earnest at age eighteen, with the December 7, 1844 copyright of "Open Thy Lattice Love," with lyrics by George P. Morris. The song was dedicated to a thirteen-year-old neighbor named Susan Pentland. In 1846 Foster's family, staunchly opposed to the idea of his embarking on a career in music, arranged for him to take a job as a bookkeeper with his brother's business in Cincinnati.

IT'S A HIT!

It is often said that American pop music was born on September 11, 1847, the day that "Oh! Susanna" was first performed. Although the first performance, given in a Pittsburgh ice cream parlor, hardly set the musical world on its ear, it did mark the beginning of a new era. In the coming months the song would be heard across the country, from stages in New York City to California mining camps. In 1849 it was reported that California gold miners, known as "forty-niners," were heard singing the song with improvised lyrics as they made their way west. Foster sold the song to W.C. Peters for the small sum of $100. Peters is said to have made over $10,000 from the tune. The success of "Oh! Susanna," a song that would still be sung generations after Foster's death, gave him the confidence to pursue his dream. In 1848 he left the bookkeeping job his family had set up for him and made his way back to Pittsburgh.

Soon after arriving in Pittsburgh, Foster teamed up with minstrel performer Ed Christy. Of the 200 or so songs that Foster wrote, about 30 of them were intended for minstrel shows. These songs were popularly referred to as "Ethiopian" songs, although they later came to be known as "plantation" songs. They were performed by white performers in "blackface." Their faces blackened with burnt cork, the performers would perform the songs in shuffling, demeaning caricatures and mockeries of the country's then enslaved African-American population. Minstrel performances were most popular in the 1830s and in the years surrounding the outbreak of the Civil War. Although separated by thirty years, the two periods of the genre's greatest popularity share an underlying theme. Both were times when much of the country's white population was troubled in conscience by the plight of the enslaved black population and even more were terribly frightened by the possibility of an uprising among the black population. The 1830 surge in minstrel popularity coincided with the bloody Nat Turner uprising, while the 1860 period coincided with political upheavals surrounding the nationally divisive issue of abolition. Through minstrel performances, the country's white population allowed itself a nervous laugh at the very subject about which it was most worried.

It has been said that Christy took Foster's pieces and passed them off as his own. In truth, Foster was hesitant about placing his name on minstrel songs, and for some time allowed Christy to use them without giving credit to the composer. It has also been said that Foster was cheated out of the rights to many of his songs and died in poverty as a result. Foster actually made some astute business deals early in his career. The machinery of publishing and promoting popular music did not yet exist in the mid-nineteenth century. It was common practice in those days for a publisher to buy the rights to a song from a composer for a small flat fee, passing none of the subsequent profits to the composer. Early in his career, Foster shrewdly worked out an arrangement with New York publisher Firth, Pond & Company that gave him a royalty for his songs rather than a flat fee. Once Christy's Minstrels introduced a Foster song, other minstrel troupes were quick to take it up. The troupes carried Foster's songs throughout the country.

MORE MINSTREL MELODIES

"Camptown Races" appeared in 1850 and became a hit on the minstrel circuit, followed by "Old Folks at Home" (or "Swanee River") in 1851. "Old Folks at Home" was something of an accidental success. Foster began writing about the Pedee River, but soon saw the poetic deficiencies of the name. After scouring maps he settled on the Swanee River in Florida, shortening it to "Swanee." Ed Christy offered Foster a small fee for the right to introduce the song and list himself as composer on printed copies of the song. Foster agreed, but kept all royalties from the sheet music sales. "Old Folks at Home" surpassed anyone's expectations for a popular song. It was reported in the 1852 *Musical World*, "...publishers keep two presses running on it, and sometimes three; yet they cannot supply the demand." "Old Folks at Home" earned Foster a sum of over $1600. It was after he saw the success of these first songs that he wrote to Christy, "I find that by my efforts I have done a great deal to build up a taste for Ethiopian songs among refined people. Therefore I have concluded to reinstate my name on my songs and pursue the Ethiopian business without fear or shame and lend all my energies to making the business live, at the same time that I will wish to establish my name as the best Ethiopian writer." Foster quickly proved himself to be "the best Ethiopian writer" with "Massa's in de Cold Ground" (1852) and "My Old Kentucky Home" (1853). After they were introduced by Christy's Minstrels, each of the songs sold over 50,000 copies. "My Old Kentucky Home" alone brought Foster over $1300 in royalties.

By the late 1840s, Foster was successfully blazing a new trail — he was making a respectable living as a writer of popular songs. In 1850 Foster married Jane Denny McDowell, the inspiration for his "Jeanie with the Light Brown Hair," which he wrote in 1854. Foster liked to tell the story that he had fallen in love with Jane's beautiful hair before he even knew her. Unfortunately, where Foster was an idealist, Jane was practical. Where Foster enjoyed a drink and a good party, Jane was a devout Methodist who disapproved of such things. Jane thought her husband ought to give up the songwriting business for something more lucrative, stable and dignified. Not surprisingly, the marriage was a failure. It was not long before the couple separated. Although they never divorced, they continued a pattern of separation and reconciliation that would continue until Foster's death.

Foster's first successful songs were either written in minstrel dialect or written about the South. In 1853 he broke that pattern with "Old Dog Tray." "Tray" quickly became one of his most successful songs. In the book *My Brother Stephen*, Foster's brother Morrison explained that the song was inspired by a "handsome setter" Stephen once owned. Foster borrowed the tune to "Old Dog Tray" from a minstrel tune he had written some years earlier. In 1860 Foster wrote one of his last and best minstrel songs, "Old Black Joe." Foster did not use the typical minstrel dialect in this song. Instead, he expressed a sense of grief and loss in a voice that Ken Emerson, author of *Doo-dah: Stephen Foster and the Rise of American Popular Culture*, called, "...closest of Foster's famous songs to the African-American spiritual." Emerson went on to say that "it approaches that tradition with sympathy and respect." A stylized version of the song reappeared near the end of the nineteenth century in an early printed collection of ragtime music. Some years later, country musician Uncle Dave Macon would revive not only "Old Black Joe," but "Oh! Susanna" and "Old Folks at Home" as well. American composer Charles Ives quoted musical themes from "Old Black Joe" in his 1915 "Elegy for Stephen Foster."

Foster's successful songs covered a wide range of topics. His 1860 "The Glendy Burk," like "Oh! Susanna" before it, was a minstrel song telling of a slave's riverboat journey. According to Morrison Foster, the 1865 song "Gentle Annie" was inspired by a tragic event. He wrote, "Once on a stormy night, a little girl sent on an errand was run over by a dray and killed. Stephen was dressed and about to go to an evening party when he learned of the tragedy. He went immediately to the little girl's father, who was a poor working man and a neighbor whom he esteemed. He gave up all thought of going to the party and remained all night with the dead child and her afflicted parents, endeavoring to afford the latter what comfort he could." An Annie Jenkins, the child of one of Foster's neighbors, was indeed struck and killed by a wagon. Foster also had a cousin, Annie Evans, who died after a long illness. Whichever Annie he had in mind, Foster composed one of his most tender pieces in her memory.

Another sentimental song, "Ah! May the Red Rose Live Alway!" was published in 1850, three months before Foster's marriage. With both lyrics and music by Foster, the sentimental song asks, "Why should the beautiful ever weep? Why should the beautiful ever die?" It is no surprise that 1862 found Foster writing martial tunes such as "We Are Coming Father Abraam, 300,000 More." The lyrics to this song first appeared in print shortly after President Lincoln issued a call for 300,000 extra troops.

BAD LUCK, BAD TIMES

In 1860 the Fosters temporarily reconciled and moved to New York City, where Foster had previously found success. Despite his accomplishments, he could no longer find a market for his songs. He wrote sentimental ballads and a few martial songs after the outbreak of the Civil War, but no one seemed interested. When Foster's popularity began to wane, he was forced to cut deals with Firth and Pond to get his music into print. Where early in his career he was able to arrange to keep the rights and royalties to songs that Firth and Pond published, by the later years of his career he was forced to sell the songs outright, sometimes for no money at all.

Foster began to run up debts borrowing money from his publisher, which eventually forced him to sign over songs in order to clear the books. He also gave them the rights to songs in trade for their printing a small number of copies. His popular "Nelly Was a Lady" brought him not a cent when he "sold" it to Firth and Pond for fifty copies of the printed sheet music. Foster turned to his brother Morrison for loans to cover the basics of room and board. Eventually Jane wrote to Morrison that Stephen "publishes once in a long while with Pond." Soon after that she took their daughter, Marion, and left New York for good, returning to Pennsylvania. Foster, however, refused to leave. Living in a dingy, rented room in the Bowery, he began drinking heavily. Despondent, he would spend days at a time in an alcohol-induced stupor, or "lost in his cups" as the polite saying went. Even his work space, a dark, ratty, back-room bar of a German liquor store, kept him near the alcohol that was destroying his health.

Sometime during the winter of 1862-63 Foster met George Cooper, an aspiring lyricist who was studying law. That winter the pair would write more than twenty songs, the first of which was "Willie Has Gone to the War." Foster used the name Willie in several sad ballads, a personal reference to the death of his own brother William. Most of the pair's songs dealt with the Civil War that raged to the south, including "When This Dreadful War Is Ended." Yet their most remarkable work is found in songs that reflect the beginnings of vaudeville, including a parody of popular songs entitled "The Song of All Songs," and the lighthearted "If You've Only Got a Moustache" and "There Are Plenty of Fish in the Sea." Cooper was as much Foster's caretaker as partner, looking after him and seeing him through illnesses and depression.

But Foster's luck had run out. At home in his rented room, on Sunday, January 10, 1864, Foster took a serious fall. Presumably inebriated, he struck either a wash basin or chamber pot, hitting it hard enough to severely gash his neck. The rooming house staff sent for both a doctor and Foster's collaborator and friend George Cooper. The physician was able to stitch the cut. Foster, however, was in a weakened physical state from repeated alcoholic binges and had lost a great deal of blood. He was taken to Bellevue, where his condition appeared to improve. Cooper contacted his family. Then on January 13, before any of his family could get to New York, Foster suddenly slumped over.

The 38-year-old songwriter was dead. The pockets of the tattered suit he was wearing when he arrived at the hospital held three pennies and a scrap of paper. On the paper, written in Foster's handwriting, were the words "dear friends and gentle hearts." It has always been assumed that this was an idea for a new song. One last song, "Beautiful Dreamer," was released by Pond (formerly Firth and Pond) following Foster's death. Although the title page declared it "the last song ever written by Stephen C. Foster, composed but a few days previous to his death," this was a deliberate lie. The publisher had bought "Beautiful Dreamer" from Foster about two years earlier and had gone so far as to have plates engraved for publication at that time. The decision to publish the song was made when other music publishers began offering posthumous forged pieces that were claimed to be Foster's last work.

Foster's sentimental, home-and-hearth songs took on new meaning in the years following the Civil War. Many of the songs found renewed popularity as both North and South longed for the innocent days before the fighting began. Well over a century after his death, some of Foster's songs remain schoolhouse and campfire standards. In 1939 Foster's story was told in the film *Swanee River*, starring Al Jolson and Don Ameche. The songwriter's story appeared on the silver screen again in 1952, with *I Dream of Jeanie*, starring Ray Middleton and Muriel Lawrence. Foster's songs have appeared in orchestral works written by various American composers, and numerous books have been written about him, including Emerson's 1997 *Doo-dah: Stephen Foster and the Rise of American Popular Culture*. But the real testament to Foster's achievement is the unabated popularity of his songs. The melodies of "Camptown Races," "Oh! Susanna," and "Old Folks at Home," as well as "Jeanie with the Light Brown Hair" and "Beautiful Dreamer," remain in the American folk/popular repertoire more than one hundred years after the untimely death of their composer.

FOSTER'S MELODIES
Nº 26.
JEANIE WITH THE LIGHT BROWN HAIR
38 Cts NETT.
Nº 22 Old Memories 25 cts. nett.
Nº 23 Little Ella " "
Nº 24 Ellen Bayne 38 cts. nett.
Nº 25 Willie "we have miss'd you" "
WRITTEN AND COMPOSED
BY
STEPHEN C. FOSTER.
PITTSBURGH.
H. KLEBER.
CINCINNATI.
COLBURN & FIELD.
NEW YORK.
PUBLISHED BY FIRTH, POND & CO. Nº 1 FRANKLIN SQUARE.
ST LOUIS.
WAKELAM & IUCHO.

AH! MAY THE RED ROSE LIVE ALWAY!

Words and Music by
STEPHEN C. FOSTER

G
D
G/D
D
die! Lend-ing a charm to ev-'ry ray that falls on her cheeks of
fear? Spread-ing their pet-als in mute de-light when morn in its ra-diance
bowers. Sad is my heart for the blight-ed plants; its pleas-ures are aye as
A
A7
D
G
A7
light, giv-ing the zeph-yr kiss for kiss, and nurs-ing the dew-drop
breaks, keep-ing a flo-ral fes-ti-val till the night-lov-ing prim-rose
brief. They bloom at the young year's joy-ful call and fade with the au-tumn
Freely
Tempo I
D
G
Em
C
bright. Ah! may the red rose live al-way, to
wakes. Long may the dai-sies dance the field,
leaf. Ah! may the red rose live al-way, to

G
D7
G
smile up - on earth and sky!
frol - ick - ing far and near.
smile up - on earth and sky.
Why should the beau - ti - ful
Why should the in - no - cent
Why should the beau - ti - ful
Em
Am/C
G/D
D7
G
ev - er weep? Why should the beau - ti - ful die?
hide their heads? Why should the in - no - cent fear?
ev - er weep? Why should the in - no - cent die?
rit.
a tempo
Gdim
G
D7
1,2
G
3
G
rit.

BEAUTIFUL DREAMER

Words and Music by
STEPHEN C. FOSTER

Fm/A♭
B♭7
heard in the day,
va - pors are borne,
lulled by the moon - light have all passed a -
wait - ing to fade at the bright com - ing
E♭
B♭7
way.
morn.
Beau - ti - ful dream - er,
Beau - ti - ful dream - er,
E♭
F7
queen of my song,
beam on my heart,
list while I woo thee with
e'en as the morn on the
B♭
E♭
soft mel - o - dy.
stream - let and sea;
Gone are the cares of
then will all clouds of

Fm/A♭
B♭7
life's bus - y throng.
sor - row de - part.
Beau - ti - ful dream - er, a - wake un - to
E♭
G7/D
Cm
A♭
E♭/B♭
B♭
E♭
me!
Beau - ti - ful dream - er, a - wake un - to
me!
rit.
a tempo
Fm/A♭
1
B♭7
E♭
2
B♭7
E♭
rit.
a tempo

BETTER TIMES ARE COMING

Words and Music by
STEPHEN C. FOSTER

Moderately, with spirit

C F/C C G/B C G C F/C C G7 C F C/G G7 C G

mf

1. There are voic - es of hope that are borne on the air, and our land will be freed from its clouds of de - spair, for brave men and true men to bat - tle have gone, and good times, good times are now com - ing on.

2. Lin - coln has the ar - my and the na - vy in his hands, while Sew - ard keeps our hon - or bright a - broad in for - eign lands and Stan - ton is a man who is stur - dy as a rock, with brave men to back him up and stand the bat - tle's shock.

3.-9. *(See additional lyrics)*

Hur - rah! Hur - rah! Hur - rah!

Additional Lyrics

3. Now McClellan is a leader and we'll let him take the sway,
For a man in his position, he should surely have his way.
Our nation's honored Scott, he has trusted to his might.
Your faith in McClellan put for we are sure he's right.

4. Generals Lyon and Baker and Ellsworth now are gone,
But we still have some brave men to lead the soldiers on.
The noise of the battle will soon have died away,
And the darkness now upon us will be turned to happy day.

5. Generals Sigel and Halleck they have conquered in the West,
And Burnside, victorious, he rides the ocean's breast.
The traitors and the rebels will soon meet their doom;
Then peace and prosperity will dwell in every home.

6. Captain Foote is commander of the Mississippi fleet,
For his flag he strikes and makes the traitors beat a quick retreat.
With iron-clad gun-boats he makes the rebels run,
While Grant makes our colors wave and glitter in the sun.

7. General Fremont the path-finder never lags behind.
He is gone to the mountains, new pathways to find.
His voice is for freedom, and his sword is for the right.
Then hail! noble Fremont, the nation's delight.

8. From the land of the shamrock there's stuff that never yields,
For we've brave Colonel Corcoran and gallant General Shields.
From Meagher soon we'll hear, for we know that he is true
And stands for the honor of the Red, White and Blue.

9. Here's health to Captain Ericsson, the Monitor and crew,
Who showed the southern chivalry a thing they never knew.
The Merrimac had slayed as St. Patrick did the toads,
'Till Worden and the Monitor came into Hampton Roads.

CAMPTOWN RACES

Words and Music by
STEPHEN C. FOSTER

A7
D
Solo:
Oh! doo - dah - day! I come down dah wid my
Oh! doo - dah - day! De blind hoss stick - en in a
Oh! doo - dah day! Den fly a - long like a
Oh! doo - dah - day! I win my mon - ey on de
A7
Chorus:
Solo:
hat caved in. Doo - dah! Doo - dah! I
big mud - hole. Doo - dah! Doo - dah!
rail - road car. Doo - dah! Doo - dah!
bob - tail nag. Doo - dah! Doo - dah! I
D
A7
D
Chorus:
go back home wid a pock-et full of tin. Oh! doo - dah - day!
Can't touch bot-tom wid a ten - foot _ pole. Oh! doo - dah - day!
Run - nin' a race wid a shoot - in' __ star. Oh! doo - dah - day!
keep my mon-ey in an old __ tow - bag. Oh! doo - dah - day!

Chorus:
G/D
D
Gwine to run all night! Gwine to run all day! I'll ___
Em/G
A7
D
bet my mon-ey on de bob - tail nag; some - bod - y bet on de bay.
Em/G
E7/G♯
A
D
A7
1-3
D
4
D
De
Old

HARD TIMES COME AGAIN NO MORE

Words and Music by
STEPHEN C. FOSTER

B♭7
E♭
A♭
song that will lin - ger for - ev - er in our ears; oh!
voic - es are si - lent, their plead - ing looks will say, "Oh!
voice would be mer - ry, 'tis sigh - ing all the day, "Oh!
dirge that is mur - mured a - round the low - ly grave; oh!
E♭/B♭
B♭7
E♭
hard times, come a - gain no more.
hard times, come a - gain no more."
hard times, come a - gain no more."
hard times, come a - gain no more.
'Tis the
A♭/E♭
E♭
song, the sigh of the wea - ry.
F7
B♭
hard times, hard times, come a - gain no more. Man - y

Eb
Bb7
Eb
Ab
days you have lin - gered a - round my cab - in door; Oh!
Eb/Bb
Bb7
Eb
hard times, come a - gain no more.
Eb/G
Fm/Ab
1-3
Eb/Bb
Bb7
8va
Eb
4
Eb/Bb
Bb7
Eb
While we
There's a
'Tis a
rit.

GENTLE ANNIE

Words and Music by
STEPHEN C. FOSTER

Ab
4 fr
Eb
3 fr
Cm
3 fr
F7
nev - er more be - hold thee nev - er hear thy win - ning voice a -
Bb
Eb
3 fr
Bb7
Eb
3 fr
Ab
4 fr
gain when the spring - time comes, gen - tle An - nie, when the
Eb/Bb
3 fr
Bb7
Eb
3 fr
Bb7
wild flowers are scat - tered o'er the plain?
Eb
3 fr
Ab
4 fr
Adim
Eb/Bb
3 fr
Bb7
1,2
Eb
3 fr
3
Eb
3 fr
We have
Ah! the
3
rit.

THE GLENDY BURK

Words and Music by
STEPHEN C. FOSTER

G D7 G D7/F# G
work too hard; I'm bound to leave dis town. I'll take my duds and tote 'em on my back when de
in - gine roars and de wheel goes round and round. So fare you well, for I'll take a lit - tle ride when de
hay - field here and knock my head wid de flail. I'll go wha day work wid de sug - ar and de cane ___ and
hon - ey dear, oh don't you fret, Miss Brown. I'll take you back 'fore de mid - dle of de week when de
G/D D7 G D7
Glen - dy Burk comes down.
Glen - dy Burk comes down.
roll on de cot - ton bale.
Glen - dy Burk comes down.
Ho! for Lou' - si - an - a! I'm bound to leave dis
G D7/F# G G/D D7 1-3 G
town. I'll take my duds and tote 'em on my back when de Glen - dy Burk comes down.
4 G G/D D7 G
down.

IF YOU'VE ONLY GOT A MOUSTACHE

Words by GEORGE COOPER
Music by STEPHEN C. FOSTER

D
A7/E
D
al - ways a chance while there's life to cap - ture the hearts of the
used to have some - thing to do with young la - dies chang - ing their
eyes may be green as the grass, your heart just as hard as a
down to the riv - er I ran to quick - ly dis - pose of my
A
D/F♯
fair. No mat - ter what may be your age, you
name. There's no rea son now to de - spond or
wall. Yet take the ad - vice that I give; you'll
woe. A good friend, he gave me ad - vice and
G
E7/G♯
A
D
Em7/D
al - ways may cut a fine dash. You will suit all the girls to a
go and do an - y - thing rash, for you'll do, though you can't raise a
soon gain af - fec - tion and cash and will be all the rage with the
time - ly pre - vent - ed the splash; now at home I've a wife and ten

D/F♯ G D/A A♯dim7 Bm G D G
hair ___ if you've on - ly got a mous-tache, a mous-tache, a mous -
cent, ___ if you'll on - ly raise a mous-tache, a mous-tache, a mous -
girls ___ if you'll on - ly get a mous-tache, a mous-tache, a mous -
heirs, ___ and all through a hand-some mous-tache, a mous-tache, a mous -
D G D/A A7 D
tache, if you've on - ly got a mous - tache. ___
tache, if you'll on - ly raise a mous - tache. ___
tache, if you'll on - ly get a mous - tache. ___
tache, and all through a hand-some mous - tache. ___
8va
G D/A A7
1-3
D
4
D
No
Your
I

JEANIE WITH THE LIGHT BROWN HAIR

Words and Music by
STEPHEN C. FOSTER

F C Dm/F
see her trip-ping where the bright streams play, hap-py as the dai - sies that
hear her mel-o-dies, like joys gone by, sigh-ing 'round my heart o'er the
smiles have van-ished and her sweet songs flown, flit-ting like the dreams that have
C/G G7 C C/B♭ F/A
dance on her way. Man-y were the wild notes her mer-ry voice would pour,
fond hopes that die. Sigh-ing like the night wind and sob-bing like the rain,
cheered us and gone. How the nod-ding wild-flowers may with-er on the shore,
B♭ F/A A Dm G7 C
ad lib.
man-y were the blithe birds that war-bled them o'er. Oh! I
wail-ing for the lost one that comes not a-gain. Oh! I
while her gen-tle fin-gers will cull them no more. Oh! I
cresc.

F
dream of Jean - ie with the light brown hair,
long for Jean - ie, and my heart bows low,
sigh for Jean - ie with the light brown hair,
mf a tempo
Dm
B♭
F/A
B♭
F/C
C7
F
float - ing like a va - por on the soft sum - mer air.
nev - er more to find her where the bright wa - ters flow.
float - ing like a va - por on the soft sum - mer air.
rallentando
B♭/F
F
1,2
F/A
B♭
8va
loco
a tempo
F/C
C7
F
I
I
3
F/A
B♭
F/C
C7
F
loco
rit.

MAGGIE BY MY SIDE

Words and Music by
STEPHEN C. FOSTER

G
C
roam with a proud heart, Mag - gie's by my side. My
p rit.
G
B7/F♯
Em
D7
own love, Mag - gie dear, sit - ting by my side;
mf a tempo
G
D7/A
G7/B
C
G/D
D7
G
Mag - gie dear, my own love, sit - ting by my side.
rit.
D7/A
G/B
C
C♯dim7
G/D
f a tempo

D
D7
G
Am/C
A7/C#
D
The wind howl-ing o'er the bil-low from the dis-tant lea, the
Storms can ap-pall me nev-er while her brow is clear,
mf
G
D7
G
storm rag-ing 'round my pil-low brings no care to me.
fair weath-er lin-gers ev-er where her smiles ap-pear.
D
Roll on, ye dark waves, o'er the trou-bled tide; I
When sor-row's break-ers 'round my heart shall hide,
f
G
C
heed not your an-ger, Mag-gie's by my side.
still may I find her sit-ting by my side.
My
p rit.

G
B7/F♯
Em
D7
own love, Mag - gie dear, sit - ting by my side;
mf a tempo
G
D7/A
G7/B
C
G/D
D7
G
Mag - gie dear, my own love, sit - ting by my side.
rit.
D7/A
G/B
C
1
C♯dim7
G/D
f a tempo
D
D7
G
2
C♯dim7
G/D
D
D7
G
rit.

MASSA'S IN DE COLD GROUND

Words and Music by
STEPHEN C. FOSTER

D
G
D/A
A7
while de mock-ing-bird am sing - ing, hap-py as de day am
hard to hear old Mas-sa call - ing cayse he was so weak and
Now dey sad-ly weep a-bove him, mourn-ing cayse he leave dem be-
D
G/D
long. Where de i-vy am a-creep - ing
old. Now de or-ange tree am bloom - ing
hind. I can - not work be-fore to-mor - row
D
A7
D
o'er de grass - y mound, dere old Mas-sa am a-
on de sand - y shore, now dc sum-mer days am
cayse de tear-drops flow. I try to drive a-way my

G
D/A
A7
D
sleep - ing, sleep - ing in de cold, cold ground.
com - ing; Mas - sa neb - ber calls no more.
sor - row pick - in' on de old ban - jo.
G
D
Down in de corn - field, hear dat mourn - ful
A7
D
G
sound. All de dark - eys am a - weep - ing;
D/A
A7
D
G
Mas - sa's in de cold, cold ground. Down in de

D
A7
corn - field, hear dat mourn - ful sound.
D
G
D/A
A7
All de dark - eys am a - weep - ing; Mas - sa's in de cold, cold
D
G
ground.
1,2
D/A
A7
D
3
D/A
A7
D
rit.

MY OLD KENTUCKY HOME

Words and Music by
STEPHEN C. FOSTER

G/D
D7
G
birds make mu - sic all the day. The young folks roll on the
bench by the old cab - in door. The day goes by like a
field where the sug - ar - canes _ grow. A few more days for to
C/G
G
A7
D
G
lit - tle cab - in floor, all mer - ry, all hap - py and bright. By'n by hard times comes a
shad - ow o'er the heart, with sor - row where all was de - light. The time has come when the
tote the wea - ry load; no mat - ter, 'twill nev - er be light. A few more days till we
C/G
G
G/D
D7
G
C/G
knock - ing at the door; then my old Ken - tuck - y home, good night!
dark - ies have to part; then my old Ken - tuck - y home, good night!
tot - ter on the road; then my old Ken - tuck - y home, good night!
Weep no more, my

G
C
G
la - dy, oh! weep no more to - day! We will sing one song for the
C/G
G
G/D
D7
1,2
G
3
G
old Ken-tuck - y home, for the old Ken-tuck - y home far a - way.
They
The
way.
C/G
D7/F#
G
D
G
C/G
G
G/D
D7
G
rit.

NOTHING BUT A PLAIN OLD SOLDIER

Words and Music by
STEPHEN C. FOSTER

C
F
C
home and my coun-try to me were dear, and I fought for both when the
tomb and the bat-tle have laid them low, and they roam no more where the
had man-y gen-'rals from o - ver the land you've tried one by one and you're
C/G
G
C
F
ad lib.
foe came near, but now I will meet with a slight or sneer, for I'm
bright streams flow. I'm long - ing to join them and soon must go, for I'm
still at a stand, but when I took the field we had one in com-mand, yet I'm
C/G
G7
C
F
C7
noth-ing but a plain old sol - dier.
noth-ing but a plain old sol - dier.
noth-ing but a plain old sol - dier.
Noth-ing but a plain old
a tempo

F
C
sol - dier, an old rev - o - lu - tion - ar - y sol - dier, but I've
F
B♭
F/C
C7
han - dled a gun where no - ble deeds were done, for the name of my com - mand - er was
F
B♭/F
F
C7
F
George Wash - ing - ton.
B♭
F/C
C
1,2
F
3
F
The
A -

MY WIFE IS A MOST KNOWING WOMAN

Words and Music by GEORGE COOPER
and STEPHEN C. FOSTER

F7/C
3fr
a - tions but in - stant - ly puts me to
from her; she knows what I do, where I
Bb
Bb7
Eb
3fr
rout. There's no use to try to de - ceive her; if
go. And if I come in af - ter mid - night and
F7
Bb
out with my friends, night or day, in the
say, "I have been to the lodge," oh, she
Bb7
Eb
3fr
Bb7/D
3fr
most in - con - ceiv - a - ble man - ner she tells where I've been right a -
says when she flies in a fu - ry, "Now don't think to play such a

E♭
3 fr
way. She says that I'm "mean" and "in -
dodge! It's all ver - y fine but won't
B♭7
hu - man." Oh! my wife is a most know - ing
do, man." Oh! my wife is a most know - ing
E♭
3 fr
B♭7
wom - an!
wom - an!
E♭/G
3 fr
F7
B♭

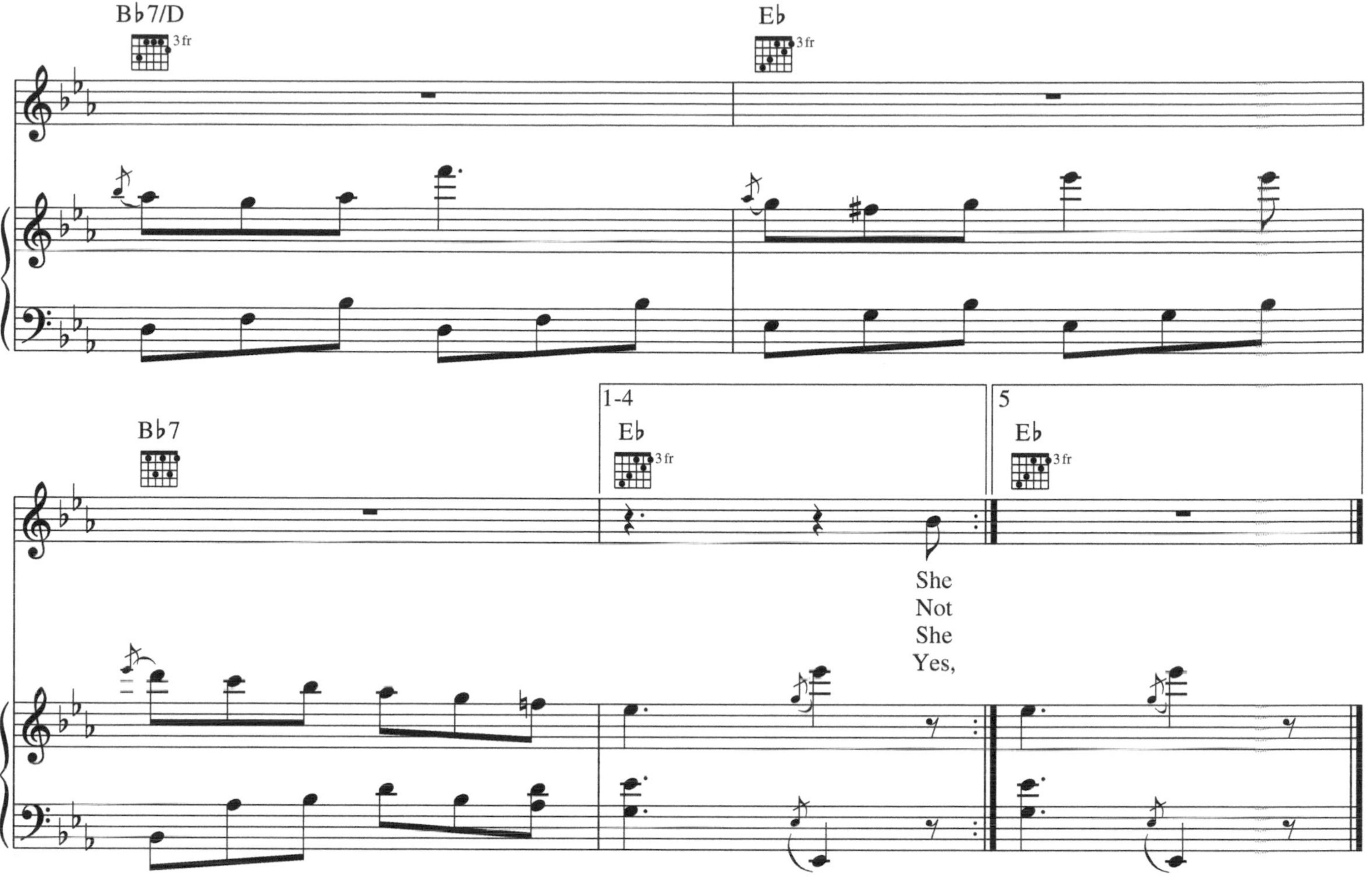

Additional Lyrics

3. Not often I go out to dinner
   And come home a little "so so."
   I try to creep up through the hallway
   As still as a mouse, on tip-toe.
   She's sure to be waiting up for me,
   And then comes a nice little scene.
   "What, you tell me you're sober, you wretch you;
   Now don't think that I am so green!
   My life is quite worn out with you, man."
   Oh, my wife is a most knowing woman!

4. She knows me much better than I do;
   Her eyes are like those of a lynx,
   Though how she discovers my secrets
   Is a riddle would puzzle a sphynx.
   On fair days, when we go out walking,
   If ladies look at me askance,
   In the most harmless way, I assure you,
   My wife gives me, oh! such a glance,
   And says, "All these insults you'll rue, man."
   Oh, my wife is a most knowing woman!

5. Yes, I must give all of my friends up
   If I would live happy and quiet.
   One might as well be 'neath a tombstone
   As live in confusion and riot.
   This life we all know is a short one,
   While some tongues are long, heaven knows,
   And a miserable life is a husband's
   Who numbers his wife with his foes.
   I'll stay at home like a true man,
   For my wife is a most knowing woman!

OH! SUSANNA

Words and Music by
STEPHEN C. FOSTER

G
Em
Am/C
G/D
D7
G
sun so hot I froze to def. Su - san - na, don't you cry.
says I'se com - ing from de Souf. Su - san - na, don't you cry.
C
G/B
G
D
G
Em
Am/C
Oh! Su - san - na, do not cry for me, I come from Al - a - bam - a wid my
G/D
D7
G
D
ban - jo on my knee.
8va
G
1
D7
G
2
D7
G
I

OLD BLACK JOE

Words and Music by
STEPHEN C. FOSTER

G/D
D
coming, I'm coming, for my head is bending low. I
A7
G
D/A
hear those gentle voices calling, "Old Black Joe."
1,2
3
rit.

OLD DOG TRAY

Words and Music by
STEPHEN C. FOSTER

Am/C
G/D
D7
G
D7
sport - ing with my old dog Tray.
Old dog Tray's ev - er
G
D7
G
faith - ful;
grief can - not drive him a - way.
He's
D7
G
Am/C
G/D
D7
gen - tle, he is kind;
I'll nev - er, nev - er find a bet - ter friend than old dog
G
D7/F#
G
D7/F#
G
Tray.

G/B
Am/C
G/D
D7
G
D7
The forms I called my own have
thoughts re - call the past, his
G
Am/C
G/D
D7
van-ished one by one; the loved ones, the dear ones have all passed a - way. Their
eyes are on me cast; I know that he feels what my break-ing heart would say. Al -
G
D7
G
Am/C
G/D
D7
hap - py smiles have flown, their gen - tle voic - es gone; I've noth-ing left but old dog
though he can - not speak, I'll vain - ly, vain - ly seek a bet - ter friend than old dog
G
D7
G
Tray.
Tray.
Old dog Tray's ev - er faith - ful;

D7
G
D7
grief can - not drive him a - way. He's gen - tle, he is kind; I'll
G
Am/C
G/D
D7
G
nev - er, nev - er find a bet - ter friend than old dog Tray.
D7/F♯
G
D7/F♯
G
1
G/B
Am/C
G/D
D7
G
When
2
G/B
Am/C
G/D
D7
G
rit.

OLD FOLKS AT HOME

Words and Music by
STEPHEN C. FOSTER

D/A
A7
D
dere's wha de old folks stay. All up and down de
man - y de songs I sung. When I was play - ing
no mat - ter where I rove. When will I see de
G/D
D
A7
whole cre - a - tion, sad - ly I roam,
wid my brud - der, hap - py was I.
bees a hum - ming all round de comb?
D
G
D/A
A7
still long - ing for de old plan - ta - tion and for de old folks at
Oh! take me to my kind old mud - der dere let me live and
When will I hear de ban - jo tum - ming down in my good old
D
A7
D
home.
die.
home?
All de world am sad and drear - y

G
D
Eb - ry - where I roam.
Oh! dark eyes, how my
G
D/A
A7
D
heart grows wea - ry, far from de old folks at home.
A7
D
G
All de world am sad and drear - y eb - ry - where I
D
G
roam.
Oh! dark - eys, how my heart grows wea - ry,

D/A
A7
far from de old folks at home.
G/D
D
A7
D
G
1,2
D/A
A7
D
3
D/A
A7
D
rit.

OPEN THY LATTICE LOVE

Words and Music by
STEPHEN C. FOSTER

A7/C♯
D
A
A7
D
G/D
D
hills with its ray, a - way o'er the wa - ters, a - way and a - way.! Then
cut the bright spray or skim like a bird o'er the wa - ters a - way. Then
G/D
D
G/D
D
o - pen thy __ lat-tice, love, lis - ten to me, while the moon's in the sky and the
o - pen thy __ lat-tice, love, lis - ten to me, while the moon's in the sky and the
A7
D
G/D
D
G/D
D
breeze on the sea.
breeze on the sea.
1
2

SOME FOLKS

Words and Music by
STEPHEN C. FOSTER

Additional Lyrics

3. Some folks fret and scold,
Some folks do, some folks do.
They'll soon be dead and cold -
But that's not me nor you.

4. Some folks get grey hairs,
Some folks do, some folks do,
Brooding o'er their cares,
But that's not me nor you.

5. Some folks toil and save,
Some folks do, some folks do,
To buy themselves a grave,
But that's not me nor you.

THE SONG OF ALL SONGS

F
B♭/F
F
up in a row. The ti - tles to read you may stand for a - while, and
Rag - ing Can-awl?" There was "Bon - nie An - nie" with "A Jock - ey Hat and Feath - er." "I Don't
Fdim
F
C
F
some are so odd they will cause you to smile. I not - ed them down as I
Think Much of You"; "We were Boys and Girls To - geth - er." "Do They Think of Me at Home?" "I'll Be
C7
F/A
Gm/B♭
C7
F
read them a - long, and I've put them to - geth - er to make up my song.
Free and Eas - y Still." "Give Us Now a Good Com-mand - er" with "The Sword of Bunk - er Hill."
B♭
F
B♭
F
C7
Old songs! New songs! Ev - 'ry kind of song! I not - ed them down as I

Additional Lyrics

3. "When This Cruel War Is Over," "No Irish Need Apply,"
"For, Everything Is Lovely, and the Goose Hangs High."
"The Young Gal from New Jersey," "Oh, Wilt Thou Be My Bride?"
And "Oft in the Stilly Night" "We'll All Take a Ride."
"Let Me Kiss Him for His Mother;" "He's a Gay Young Gambolier."
"I'm Going to Fight Mit Sigel" and "De Bully Lager-bier."
"Hunkey Boy Is Yankee Doodle" "When the Cannons Loudly Roar"
"We Are Coming, Father Abraham, Six Hundred Thousand More!"

4. "In the Days When I Was Hard Up" with "My Mary Ann,"
"My Johnny Was a Shoemaker," or "Any Other Man!"
"The Captain with His Whiskers" and "Annie of the Vale,"
Along with "Old Bob Ridley," "A Riding on a Rail!"
"Rock Me to Sleep, Mother," "Going Round the Horn;"
"I'm Not Myself at All," "I'm a Bachelor Forlorn."
"Mother, Is the Battle Over?" "What Are the Men About?"
"How Are You, Horace Greeley," "Does Your Mother Know You're Out?"

5. "We Won't Go Home Till Morning," with "The Bold Privateer,"
"Annie Lisle" and "Zouave Johnny" "Riding in a Railroad Kerr."
"We Are Coming, Sister Mary," with "The Folks That Put on Airs."
"We Are Marching Along" with "The Four-and-Thirty Stars."
"On the Other Side of Jordan," "Don't Fly Your Kite Too High!"
"Jenny's Coming O'er the Green" to "Root Hog or Die!"
"Our Union's Starry Banner," "The Flag of Washington,"
Shall float victorious o'er the land from Maine to Oregon!

THERE ARE PLENTY OF FISH IN THE SEA

Words and Music by GEORGE COOPER
and STEPHEN C. FOSTER

F
C/G
G7
laughed to scorn the vows from hearts though false or
care - less life she led, and was not yet a
beaux had grown quite shy; her face no long - er
C
Am
E7
true, while mer - ri - ly she sang and
bride. Still as of old she sang, though
charmed. And now she sad - ly sings the
Am
D7
G
C
cared all day for naught. There are plen - ty of fish in the
few to win her sought. There are plen - ty of fish in the
les - son time has taught: There are plen - ty of fish in the
F
C/G
G7
C
sea, as good as ev - er were caught. There are
sea, as good as ev - er were caught. There are
sea, but oh, they're hard to be caught. There are

G7/B
Am
F♯dim7
C/G
G7
plen - ty of fish in the sea, as good as ev - er were
plen - ty of fish in the sea, as good as ev - er were
plen - ty of fish in the sea, but oh, they're hard to be
C
F/C
caught.
caught.
caught.
C
G7/B
C
G/B
C
F
Dm/F
C/G
G7
1,2
C
3
C
Up
At

THAT'S WHAT'S THE MATTER

Words and Music by
STEPHEN C. FOSTER

Additional Lyrics

3. The Rebels thought we would divide
   And Democrats would take their side;
   They then would let the Union slide,
   And that's what's the matter!
   But when the war had once begun,
   All party feeling soon was gone;
   We joined as brothers, ev'ryone,
   And that's what's the matter!

4. The Merrimac, with heavy sway,
   Had made our fleet an easy prey.
   The Monitor got in the way,
   And that's what's the matter!
   So health to Captain Ericsson;
   I cannot tell all he has done,
   I'd never stop when once begun,
   And that's what's the matter!

5. We've heard of Gen'ral Beauregard,
   And thought he'd fight us long and hard,
   But he has played out his last card,
   And that's what's the matter!
   So what's the use to fret and pout,
   We soon will hear the people shout,
   "Secession dodge is all played out!"
   And that's what's the matter!

THERE'S A GOOD TIME COMING

Words and Music by
STEPHEN C. FOSTER

F
C7
F
may not live to see the day, but earth shall glis - ten in the ray
pen shall su - per-sede the sword and right, not might, shall be the lord
rit.
C7
F
of the good time ___ com - ing.
in the good time ___ com - ing.
accel.
B♭
F7
B♭
Can - non - balls may aid the truth, but thought's a wea - pon strong - er. We'll
Worth, not birth, shall rule man-kind and be ac - knowl-edged strong - er. The
mf a tempo
E♭/B♭
B♭
B♭/F
F7
B♭
3fr
win our bat - tle by its aid; wait a lit - tle long - er.
prop er im - pulse has been giv'n; wait a lit - tle long - er.
f

Additional Lyrics

3. There's a good time coming, boys,
A good time coming,
A good time coming.
War in all men's eyes shall be.
A monster of iniquity.
In the good time coming.
Nations shall not quarrel then
To prove which is the stronger,
Nor slaughter men for glory's sake;
Wait a little longer.

4. There's a good time coming, boys,
A good time coming,
A good time coming.
Shameful rivalries of creed
Shall not make the martyr bleed
In the good time coming.
Religion shall be shorn of pride
And flourish all the stronger,
And Charity shall trim her lamp;
Wait a little longer.

5. There's a good time coming, boys,
A good time coming,
A good time coming.
And a poor man's family
Shall not be his misery
In the good time coming.
Ev'ry child shall be a help
To make his right arm stronger.
The happier he, the more he has;
Wait a little longer.

6. There's a good time coming, boys,
A good time coming,
A good time coming.
Little children shall not toil
Under or above the soil
In the good time coming,
But shall play in healthful fields
Till limbs and minds grow stronger,
And ev'ryone shall read and write;
Wait a little longer.

7. There's a good time coming, boys,
A good time coming,
A good time coming.
The people shall be temperate
And shall love instead of hate
In the good time coming.
They shall use and not abuse
And make all virtue stronger.
The reformation has begun;
Wait a little longer.

8. There's a good time coming, boys,
A good time coming,
A good time coming.
Let us aid it all we can,
Ev'ry woman, ev'ry man,
The good time coming.
Smallest helps, if rightly giv'n,
Make the impulse stronger.
'Twill be strong enough one day;
Wait a little longer.

THOU ART THE QUEEN OF MY SONG

Words and Music by
STEPHEN C. FOSTER

G7 C G7/B
sigh for thee; will thou come not back a - gain? Though cold forms sur-round us to
days of love we so fond - ly whiled a - way. But still while I'm dream - ing, thy
turn to thee, and my sad - dest thoughts are gone, for love will be burn - ing and
C Dm/F G7 C
sev - er all that bound us, gen - tle queen _ of my song. The
smiles are o'er me beam - ing, gen - tle queen _ of my song. The
mem - 'ry still re - turn - ing, gen - tle queen _ of my song.
F C F
fields and the fair flowers shall wel - come thee, and all to thy pleas-ures shall be -
wind o'er the lone mead - ow wails for thee, the birds sing thy beau - ties all day
Come let thy warm heart re - joice with me, come from the bright and lur - ing
C E7/G# Am Dm/F
long. Pride of my ear - ly years,
long. Pride of my ear - ly years,
throng. Pride of my ear - ly years,

C/G
G7
C
G7
thou art the queen of my song.
thou art the queen of my song.
thou art the queen of my song.
C
F
C
E7/G♯
Am
Dm/F
1,2
C/G
G7
C
The
I
3
C/G
G7
C
rit.

THE VILLAGE MAIDEN

Words and Music by
STEPHEN C. FOSTER

Moderately

D G/D D

mf

D/F# Em7/G D/A A7 D

The vil - lage bells are
sum - mer joys have
vil - lage bells are

G/D D

ring - ing, and mer - ri - ly they chime; the vil - lage choir is
fad - ed, and sum - mer hopes have flown; her brow with grief is
ring - ing, but hark, how sad and slow; the vil - lage choir is

G/D D

sing - ing, for 'tis a hap - py time. The chap - el walls are
shad - ed, her hap - py smiles are gone. Yet why her heart is
sing - ing a re - quiem soft and low, and all with sor - row

A7/E
D7/F#
G
D/F#
la - den with gar - lands rich and gay to greet the vil - lage
la - den, not one, a - las! can say, who saw the vil - lage
la - den their tear - ful trib - ute pay, who saw the vil - lage
Em/G
D/A
A7
D
A7/E
maid - en up - on her wed-ding day.
maid - en up - on her wed - ding day.
maid - en up - on her wed - ding day.
D7/F#
G
D/F#
1,2
Em7/G
D/A
A7
D
But
The
3
Em7/G
D/A
A7
D
rit.

THE VOICES THAT ARE GONE

Words and Music by
STEPHEN C. FOSTER

F
past be - fore me, joys and sor - rows,
light - ly fall - ing, come the voic - es
vain re - gret - ting o - ver mem - 'ries
C
Cdim
smiles and tears. Then a - gain bright
that are gone. Voic - es heard in
I would shun. But when death is
C
eyes are gleam - ing with the love once
days of child - hood soft - ly at the
o'er to meet me, may some much - loved
F6
C
in them shone; then, like mu - sic
hour of prayer or loud ring - ing
forms come on, and the first sounds

G7
heard when dream - ing, come the voic - es
through the wild - wood when the young heart
that shall greet me be the voic - es
C
that are gone.
knew no care.
that were gone.
Once a - gain bright
D7/A
G7
eyes are gleam - ing with the light that
C
in them shone; then, like mu - sic

C/G
G7
heard when dream - ing, come the voic - es
C
that are gone.
rit.
1,2
G7
C
3
G7
C
rit.

WE ARE COMING, FATHER ABRAAM, 300,000 MORE

Words and Music by
STEPHEN C. FOSTER

G
leave our plows and work - shops, our wives and chil - dren dear, with
now the wind and in - stant tears the cloud - y veil a - side and
chil - dren from their moth - ers' knees are pull - ing at the weeds and
from foul trea - son's sav - age group to wrench the mur - d'rous blade, and
C F C/G G7 C
hearts too full for ut - ter - ance, with but a si - lent tear. We
floats a - loft our span - gled flag to glo - ry and in pride, and
learn - ing how to reap and sow a - gainst their coun - try's needs, and a
in the face of for - eign foes its frag - ments to pa - rade. Six
G7 C D7 G
dare not look be - hind us, but stead - fast - ly be - fore. We are
bay - o - nets in the sun - light gleam, and bands 'brave mu - sic pour. We are
fare - well group stands weep - ing at ev - 'ry cot - tage door. We are
hun - dred thou - sand loy - al men and true have gone be - fore. We are
C F C/G G7 C
com - ing, Fa - ther A - braam, three hun - dred thou - sand more.
com - ing, Fa - ther A - braam, three hun - dred thou - sand more.
com - ing, Fa - ther A - braam, three hun - dred thou - sand more.
com - ing, Fa - ther A - braam, three hun - dred thou - sand more.
We are

F C G
com - ing, com - ing, our un - ion to re - store; we are
C F C/G G7 C
com - ing, Fa - ther A - braam, with three hun - dred thou - sand more.
F C G C
Dm/F C/G G7
1-3 C
4 C
If you
If you
You have

WHEN THIS DREADFUL WAR IS ENDED

Words and Music by GEORGE COOPER
and STEPHEN C. FOSTER

G
D
wan - der, still your mem - 'ry pure and bright in my heart will ev - er
an - gel you will turn my grief to bliss; on my pale and fe - vered
meet you when the threat - 'ning storm is past and the flag our foes have
A7
D
A
lin - ger, shin - ing with un - dy - ing light. Do not weep, love, sit be -
fore - head I will of - ten feel your kiss. Our dear na - tive land's in
plant - ed flies in shreds up - on the blast. Fare - well! fare - well! best and
Bm/D
E7
A
A/C#
side me, whis - per gen - tle words of cheer; be not mourn - ful now, my
dan - ger, and we'll calm - ly bide the time till this dread - ful war is
dear - est, do not let your heart re - pine; though the sky may now look
D
A/E
E7
A
Bm/D
dar - ling, let me kiss a - way each tear.
o - ver and the bells of peace shall chime.
gloom - y, soon the sun will bright - ly shine.

E7
A
D
A7
How_ hap-py I will feel if I but know That you'll con - tent - ed
be, I'll _ nev-er, nev-er have one pang of woe while you are true to me.
D/F♯
Em/G
1,2
3
On the
When this

WILLIE HAS GONE TO THE WAR

Words and Music by GEORGE COOPER
and STEPHEN C. FOSTER

Eb Ab6 Eb/Bb Bb7 Eb
play, and soft is the sigh of the gale. I
foe, oh! dear - ly I love the old place. The
glade on fai - ry - like pin - ions will fly, and
Cm G7 Cm F7
stray by the brook - side a - lone, where oft we have wan - dered be -
whis - per - ing wa - ters re - peat the name that I love o'er and
still I will hope - ful - ly wait the day when these bat - tles are
Bb Eb Ab/Eb Eb
fore, and weep for my loved one, my own; my
o'er, and dai - sies that nod at my feet say,
o'er and pine like a bird for its mate till
Ab6 Abm6 Eb/Bb Bb7 Eb
Deliberately
Wil - lie has gone to the war!
"Wil - lie has gone to the war!"
Wil - lie comes home from the war.
Wil - lie has gone to the

A♭
E♭
F7/C
B♭
war, Will - ie, Wil - lie, my loved one my own.
E♭
A♭
E♭/B♭
B♭7
Wil - lie has gone _ to the war, Wil - lie, Wil - lie, my loved _ one, is
E♭
B♭7/F
E♭/G
A♭
Adim7
gone.
8va
f
E♭/B♭
B♭7
1,2
E♭
3
E♭
'Twas
The